SAVING OUR WORLD

CLIMATE CRISIS

Nigel Hawkes

COPPER BEECH BOOKS

BROOKFIELD, CONNECTICUT

© Aladdin Books Ltd 2000
Designed and produced by
Aladdin Books Ltd
28 Percy Street
London W1P 0LD

First published in the United States in 2000 by
Copper Beech Books,
an imprint of
The Millbrook Press
2 Old New Milford Road
Brookfield, Connecticut 06804

Editor: Kathy Gemmell
Designer: Flick Killerby
Picture Research: Brooks Krikler Research
Certain illustrations have appeared in earlier books created by Aladdin Books.

Cataloging-in-Publication data is available from the Library of Congress.
ISBN 0-7613-1155-6

Author Nigel Hawkes is science editor for *The Times* newspaper in London, England. He has written a number of books for children on a variety of science subjects.

Consultant Francis Wilson, CMet, is senior meteorologist for BSkyB Television in London, England. He has collaborated on a number of weather books for children.

ABOUT THIS BOOK

This book is divided into chapters that guide the reader through the topic. First we examine how climate has changed over the centuries and the importance of the sun to all life on Earth. We then look at the greenhouse effect and global warming, and their causes. We discuss monitoring systems and the specific effects of global warming on climate. Finally, we learn about what is being done to slow the climate crisis on our planet. Throughout the book, stimulating **Talking Points** raise greater awareness and provoke discussion about the important environmental topics and issues covered in this book. These are reinforced at the end of the book by a **Look Back and Find** section, where questions test the reader's newfound knowledge of the subject and encourage further thought and discussion.

CONTENTS

p. 4-5   Heading for Crisis

Our climate appears to be getting warmer – with potentially disastrous results.

● ● ●

CHAPTER 1: A CHANGING CLIMATE

p. 6-7   Past climates

Was there a time when the world was much colder?

p. 8-9   The sun

How much does the earth need the sun?

● ● ●

CHAPTER 2: EARTH IN THE GREENHOUSE

p. 10-11   The earth's atmosphere

What does the atmosphere have to do with greenhouses?

p. 12-13   Disturbing the balance

How are human activities changing the composition of the atmosphere?

p. 14-15   Who is to blame?

Who is producing too much carbon dioxide, and where?

p. 16-17   How do we know the earth is getting warmer?

Where does our weather information come from?

● ● ●

CHAPTER 3: WORLD WEATHER ON THE MOVE

p. 18-19   Bad weather ahead

What kind of weather does a warmer climate have in store for us?

p. 20-21   Wetter and drier

What is El Niño? What does it do to weather around the world?

p. 22-23   Rising sea levels

Why will sea levels rise? What might the effects of rising sea levels be around the world?

● ● ●

CHAPTER 4: WHAT IS BEING DONE?

p. 24-25   Alternative energy

How can we get power without adding to the warming of the atmosphere?

p. 26-27   International cooperation

Find out what is being done all over the world to address our climate problems.

● ● ●

p. 28-29   Look Back and Find

Test yourself to see how much you know about the changing climate.

● ● ●

p. 30   You Be Environmental!

Learn how you can help slow the climate crisis.

● ● ●

p. 31   GLOSSARY

● ● ●

p. 32   INDEX

Heading for Crisis

The weather is changing all the time, from day to day and from season to season. Summers are generally warm, winters are cold, and temperatures change quickly, sometimes even from hour to hour. But although weather varies in each place, the climate – the pattern of weather over months and years – has, until now, remained the same. This means that, on average, each year has had roughly the same amount of sunshine and storms. But this is now changing. Scientists now know that, as a direct result of human activities, the earth's climate is slowly but steadily getting warmer. This is affecting the regularity and strength of both our sunshine and our storms.

Global warming could drastically change climate patterns around the world, causing some areas to dry up and others to suffer increasingly bad storms.

Pollution from cities and industry causes heavy smog. Pollution is also responsible for increasing the amount of carbon dioxide in the atmosphere, which is having a great effect on our climate.

The atmosphere that surrounds the earth is made up of various gases. These gases keep the earth from becoming too cold for life – including humans – to survive. Gases that are pumped into the air by industry, cars, and homes are gradually changing the balance of gases in the earth's atmosphere. They are causing more heat from the sun to be trapped in the atmosphere than before, which is making the planet warmer. This is what is known as global warming.

The global increase in temperature is tiny compared to day-to-day variation – on average over the whole world, there has been no more than a few degrees rise in the past century. This is so small that it is hard to detect with certainty. However, there has been enough of an increase for most scientists to be convinced that the climate is changing. One result of higher global temperatures is a rise in sea levels. If this continues, the effects on low-lying countries, and especially on farming, could be catastrophic.

CHAPTER ONE

A Changing Climate

Past climates

Throughout history, natural astronomical movements have caused both hotter and colder climates on Earth. Ten thousand years ago, ice sheets called glaciers covered up to thirty percent of the earth's land surface, including much of Europe and North America. As the glaciers melted, sea levels rose, and the land took the form it has today.

The blue shows the extent of glaciers (ice sheets) 10,000 years ago.

18,000 years ago

Today

A small temperature increase has a huge effect. On average, it is only 10° warmer today than it was 18,000 years ago, yet this has been enough to melt much of the Arctic icecap.

Ice ages

Today, about a tenth of the earth's surface is covered with ice, which stores three quarters of the fresh water on Earth. But in the past two million years there have been at least fifteen ice ages, called glaciations, when the ice has spread much farther. The last retreat of the ice, ten thousand years ago, marked the birth of civilization. The warmest period was from six thousand to three thousand years ago, when temperatures may have been 4° higher than today's. It is thought that the woolly mammoth (left) died out during one of these climate changes, as vegetation changed, making food hard to find.

▼ Tree rings

Trees can live for thousands of years. The oldest bristlecone pines in North America are four thousand years old. Their growth rings – one each year – store information about temperature and rainfall. By studying these rings, scientists can plot climate variations back for thousands of years.

Changing landscapes

As the climate changed, enormous glaciers flowed downhill, leaving behind them U-shaped valleys with heaps of rock, called moraines, piled up along the edges and at the leading edge. This shaped the landscape, forming many of our steep valleys. Today, there are still glaciers in polar regions, and alpine glaciers can be seen in high mountainous areas.

An alpine glacier carves a passage through rock, forming a valley with moraines at its edges.

Meltwater

Moraine

Huge areas of floating sea ice in the Arctic are melting each year. Sea ice plays an important role in reflecting sunlight back into space.

Q: What are the likely effects of Arctic sea ice melting?

A: As more sea ice is lost, less sunlight is reflected back into space. This means that more sunlight is absorbed by the earth, and the earth heats up. Loss of sea ice is also likely to threaten polar bears who live and hunt on the ice.

The sun

The earth orbits (circles) the sun, ninety-three million miles away. All the energy that makes the earth habitable comes from the sun. The energy reaching us varies according to complex astronomical cycles that act over thousands of years. These are responsible for altering the earth's temperature enough to create ice ages.

Sunscreen protects us from harmful solar radiation.

▼ The sun

The energy that powers the sun comes from the burning of a gas called hydrogen, which forms a gas called helium at the sun's core. The sun has been burning for five billion years. When all its fuel is used up – in another five billion years – it will die, and life on Earth will die, too. Before then, gradual changes in the earth's orbit may change the effect the sun has on the earth.

Spots on the surface of the sun are temporary cooler patches. Sunspots can be thousands of miles wide.

Life's dependency ▲

The earth lies just far enough from the sun for its temperature to be ideal for life. Water can exist on the earth as a liquid and as a gas called water vapor. Plants need sunlight and water for growth (see page 11). Green plants give us our food and also produce the oxygen we need to breathe. Without the sun to help plants grow and to provide enough warmth for plants and animals to survive, life would be impossible.

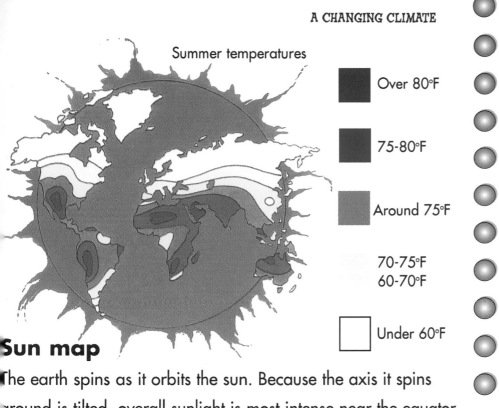

Summer temperatures

Over 80°F

75-80°F

Around 75°F

70-75°F
60-70°F

Under 60°F

Sun map

The earth spins as it orbits the sun. Because the axis it spins around is tilted, overall sunlight is most intense near the equator – around the middle of the earth – and least intense at the poles, where the sunlight hits the earth at an angle. The regions between, called temperate areas, have moderate temperatures, ample rainfall, and marked differences between the seasons.

Global change

The sun has a much greater influence on climate than humans ever will. Changes in the sun have affected the earth's climate in the past. But now, heavier rains (right) and fires caused by heatwaves (above) are being blamed not on the sun, whose output has changed little for a century, but on pollution caused by people.

TALKING POINT

All stars, including the sun, which is a fairly average star, follow a life cycle. Astronomers understand this very well from observing stars of all ages in the sky.

Q: When will the sun die?

A: When it runs out of hydrogen fuel, the sun's core will shrink and its outer layers will puff out to form a giant red star. The core will eventually form a white dwarf star, shining weakly as it cools down. But this won't happen for billions of years.

Q: Will this affect life on Earth?

A: There will be no life on Earth when the sun dies. To grow, all plants need the sun, and all animals – including humans – need both sunlight and plants because they produce our oxygen and our food.

CHAPTER TWO

Earth in the Greenhouse

The earth's atmosphere

The earth's atmosphere acts like the glass in a greenhouse, keeping the earth about 60° warmer than it would otherwise be. Without the greenhouse effect, there would be a permanent ice age. Life would be impossible.

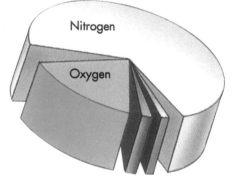

The earth's atmosphere consists mainly of nitrogen and oxygen, together with smaller amounts of greenhouse gases.

Venus has a runaway greenhouse effect. It holds a lot of CO_2 in its atmosphere and has a surface temperature of about 930°F.

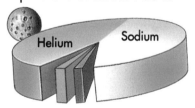

Mercury is the planet closest to the sun. Helium and sodium in its atmosphere keep the heat in.

Pluto is farthest from the sun. It does not have much atmosphere to stay warm, so it is very cold.

◄ Greenhouse gases

Greenhouse gases in the earth's atmosphere – water vapor, carbon dioxide (CO_2), methane, nitrous oxide, and ozone – are present in much smaller amounts than the main gases, nitrogen and oxygen. These greenhouse gases act like a blanket over the earth, trapping some of the earth's heat within the atmosphere. This keeps the earth extra warm, but too many greenhouse gases will make the earth overheat. The greenhouse effect also exists on other planets.

Radiation from the sun

Greenhouse gases

Heat is kept in the earth's atmosphere.

▲ Greenhouse effect

Sunlight reaching Earth passes easily through the atmosphere because it has a short wavelength. Heat sent out from Earth into space has a long wavelength. Some of this heat is absorbed by greenhouse gases and sent back to Earth, keeping it warm.

Plants absorb CO_2 from the atmosphere and use the sun's energy to turn it into carbohydrates, such as sugar and starch. As part of the process, they give off oxygen, which we breathe.

Oxygen

Carbon dioxide (CO_2)

Carbohydrates

Minerals and water

◀ Water cycle

Water vapor in the air is a powerful greenhouse gas. Heat from the sun makes water evaporate from seas and lakes. The vapor rises, cools, and condenses into tiny droplets. The droplets form clouds, then fall as rain. Clouds are nature's way of limiting temperature rises. In hotter weather, more water vapor is created, so more clouds form and more rain falls.

TALKING POINT

In the solar system, the planets on either side of the earth are Venus and Mars. Mars is cold, with an average temperature at the surface of at least −70°F. But Venus is hot, with a temperature of about 930°F.

Q: Why is the earth so different from its neighboring planets?

A: The evolution of life on Earth has created an atmosphere that has just the right balance of gases to maintain an average surface temperature of 60°. This is an ideal temperature for life. The atmosphere on Mars is too thin to retain heat, while the atmosphere on Venus is too dense, making it hot. Neither is habitable. Another essential difference is that there is enough water in the earth's atmosphere to sustain life.

Disturbing the balance

Over the past two centuries, human activities have begun to disturb the balance of gases in the earth's atmosphere by adding more greenhouse gases, particularly carbon dioxide (CO_2). This change in the atmosphere has produced a measurable rise in global temperatures.

Coal-, oil-, and gas-powered industries increase greenhouse gases.

Artificial carbon dioxide emissions

Homes

Industry

Transportation   Deforestation   Electricity

Pollutants ▲

Burning fossil fuels, which are carbon-based fuels such as coal and oil, produces CO_2. As human populations and activity expand, so do the amounts of CO_2 produced. CO_2 is the most widespread, fastest-growing greenhouse gas in the atmosphere.

Domestic heating that burns coal, oil, and gas adds more CO_2.

◀ Rice paddies

Rice paddies give off methane gas. Methane is also produced by rotting garbage and animals' digestive systems. As populations have grown, so has the amount of methane produced, and it is thirty times as powerful a greenhouse gas as CO_2. However, there are relatively tiny amounts of methane in the atmosphere compared to CO_2.

Volcanic disturbances

Volcanic eruptions can upset the climate by pumping huge amounts of gas and dust into the upper atmosphere. Sulfate particles affect temperatures most, as they reflect sunlight back to space and cause the earth to cool. But the effects are only short-term. At Mount Pinatubo in the Philippines in 1991, the dust cut the sunlight reaching the earth by two percent. This reduced temperatures by just 0.45° for two years.

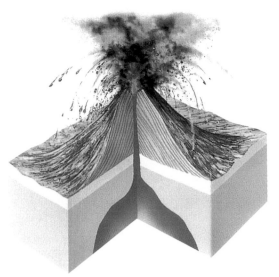

Cars, buses, and trucks all burn carbon-based fuels and produce carbon dioxide in their exhausts.

Deforestation

Plants absorb carbon dioxide and produce oxygen. This means that the destruction of forests, which is being done in many places to open up new farmland, has a triple effect. It produces CO_2 by the burning of trees and scrub, it reduces the ability of the earth to soak up excess CO_2, and it produces less oxygen as more trees are destroyed.

Developments in agriculture over many years have added to the destruction of forests. Today's need for land to grow food for rising population is responsible for most of it.

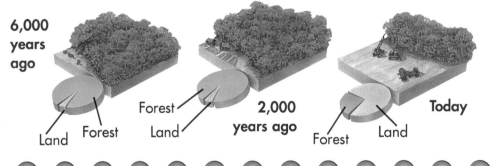

6,000 years ago   Forest   Land   Forest

2,000 years ago   Forest   Land   Today   Forest   Land

TALKING POINT

For many, many centuries, CO_2 made up a tiny proportion of the earth's atmosphere – only about 0.028 percent. This is about 280 parts per million.

Q: How do we know that CO_2 is increasing, and how fast?

A: Measurements made in Hawaii last century have shown a steady rise in CO_2 in the atmosphere, at about three parts per million per year. It has now reached more than 360 parts per million.

Who is to blame?

Carbon emissions are growing more than ever before all over the world. Developed regions such as the United States and Western Europe are by far the greatest producers of greenhouse gases because they burn far more fuel per person. But people in poorer countries need more energy to improve their quality of life, and these countries are likely to produce more and more CO_2.

Where does CO_2 come from?

More than three quarters of carbon emissions comes from burning fuel. This is divided equally among vehicles, industry, homes, and the generation of electricity. Forest-burning is responsible for the rest. Air pollution such as smog can be controlled, but cutting the production of carbon dioxide requires a huge change in human behavior.

Location statistics

The United States heads the list for CO_2 production since it is both wealthy and wasteful. Countries in Western Europe, with the same population, create far less, but still produce far more CO_2 than many developing countries put together.

Worldwide carbon emissions in millions of tons

- Canada — 105.6
- USA — 1,224.0
- Brazil
- Latin America — 229.7
- Europe — 791.6
- Former USSR — 1,103.6
- Middle East — 146.0
- Africa — 50.2
- India — 152.6
- China — 355.2
- Japan — 247.5
- Australasia — 314.7
- 365.7
- 150.4

Developing countries

In poor, developing countries, forests are cleared to provide space for farming. These countries need to do this both to feed their people and to clear their debts to richer countries by exporting food. Countries like China are increasingly adopting Western habits, which will make CO_2 emissions even worse. Also, unlike the West, poor countries cannot afford cleaner technologies that produce less CO_2.

Population growth

The world's population, now six billion, is likely to reach at least nine billion before it stops growing. Providing a decent life for so many without adding to the problems of global warming will be extremely difficult.

TALKING POINT Humans have existed for at least a hundred thousand years without having any effect on the climate – until now.

Q: Why has global warming only become a problem over the last century?

A: Because of the Industrial Revolution in the early nineteenth century: the invention of machines that made manufacturing possible and the increase of mechanized transportation greatly increased fuel consumption. Burning wood as a fuel, which people have been doing for centuries, does not cause global warming because it only releases the carbon captured by the trees. As long as more trees are planted, the balance can be maintained. But burning coal, oil, and gas releases carbon stored by plants over millions of years, and we are burning it in just a few centuries.

How do we know the earth is getting warmer?

Global records of temperature have been kept for long enough to show a small upward change of about 1°F over the last century. Almost all climate experts believe that global warming is taking place.

Evidence in nature

Studies of insects, birds, and plants all suggest that climate is changing. Birds nest earlier, while records of butterflies show they have gradually moved north during this century. The growing season for plants is steadily getting longer, while glaciers throughout Europe, particularly in the Alps, are shrinking fast.

As temperatures rise, the migration patterns of some birds are changing, with more birds able to stay longer in their summer homes before having to fly to warmer places for the winter.

Stevenson screens are mini weather stations used to house measuring devices such as thermometers.

▲ Evidence on the ground

Temperatures measured at weather stations have shown an increase over the last century. But it has not been steady, and volcanic eruptions have interfered. Cities, which produce local rises in temperature called heat islands, make it hard to be precise about global temperature readings.

▼ Evidence from the ice

Ice cores show increasing levels of CO_2 in air bubbles trapped in the ice. Observations of the ancient ice sheets in Antarctica show that some areas are melting rapidly. Some claim that global warming is speeding up the melting process.

Air bubble

Ice core

Scientists use drills to extract cores of ancient ice.

Weather satellites scan the earth below, sensing heat radiation and light reflected from the earth into space.

Evidence from space

Geostationary satellites orbit the earth every 24 hours – the same time as the earth takes to spin on its axis. This means that they are always above the same spot on Earth. They send temperature records and pictures of weather systems back to weather stations on Earth. Satellite records do not yet go far back enough to show any real climate trends.

Evidence in the atmosphere

Temperature measurements in the stratosphere, which is the part of the atmosphere where jet planes such as the

Concorde fly, show that it has been gradually cooling over recent years. This confirms that global warming is caused by CO_2 and other greenhouse gas contamination from the earth, and not by an increase in the sun's heat. If the sun were to blame, the stratosphere would be heating up as well.

TALKING POINT The evidence is that temperatures have increased by about 1° over the last century, although there was a period between 1940 and 1970 when the earth seemed to be getting cooler.

Q: How do we know what is going to happen in the future? Is global warming definitely going to continue or might there be another ice age?

A: Scientists have created computer models that work out likely future temperatures based on the expected amounts of greenhouse gases. These predict that temperatures will rise about 2° every fifty years.

CHAPTER THREE

World Weather on the Move

Bad weather ahead

A small temperature increase of about 2° every half century does not sound like much. But average temperatures in the last ice age were only 7° colder than today's temperatures. So even a tiny difference is enough to bring extreme changes in the weather. Global warming does not necessarily mean more sunshine.

Hurricanes

Hurricanes, also called typhoons in some parts of the world, can only form when sea surface temperatures reach more than 80°F. Global warming is likely to make such warm sea conditions much more common. Hurricanes are fueled by energy from the warm sea, and their paths follow the warm sea currents. Warmer seas farther north may extend hurricane paths into areas that have never experienced them before. The increase in heat and energy will also create much bigger hurricanes that do far more damage with their ferocious winds.

Hurricane clouds form a huge swirl around a central hole called the eye. Hurricane winds can reach more than 100 miles per hour.

A hailstorm with giant hailstones killed 92 people in Bangladesh in 1986. Freak weather such as this is likely to increase with global warming.

▼ Storms

Globally, the 1990s were the hottest decade ever recorded, with temperature records broken year after year. High temperatures may make some places more productive, and many places more arid (very dry), but warmer weather will also increase the frequency of storms in temperate regions. Storms in Europe in December 1999 caused enormous damage for areas not used to such bad weather. Tropical storms in often-hit places like eastern India and Florida are getting worse, with many people made homeless and extensive damage to property.

Some will benefit from global warming, while others will lose. Those in cold areas like Siberia will find that agriculture is possible, while those living close to the Sahara Desert may find the sand creeping closer.

Q: Does global warming really matter? The temperature increase will be very slow, and may even help in places.

A: The damage is likely to be much greater than the benefits because people have settled in areas that are productive and fertile. They cannot simply move, like birds or insects, to keep pace with the climate change. Certain areas of the world, like the American Midwest, are vitally important in growing enough grain to help keep the world fed. Changes that reduce output in these areas would be disastrous.

Wetter and drier

Global warming may already be making natural climatic extremes more intense. A cycle of currents in the Pacific Ocean, called El Niño, has been causing shifts in climate for years. As a result of recent global warming, El Niño now appears to be reaching greater extremes, causing a lot of damage and loss of life.

In a normal year, winds blow warm surface waters in the Pacific Ocean west. The warm water evaporates to produce clouds and rain over Australia.

El Niño

In an El Niño year, strong currents and weak winds push warm water east instead of west.

Storm clouds produce rain that would normally fall over Australia.

AUSTRALIA

SOUTH AMERICA

WEST

PACIFIC OCEAN

EAST

Water in the west is cooler than usual, and no rain is produced.

Warm water in the east evaporates to create storm clouds.

El Niño and fishing ▼

El Niño ("the little boy") often appears off the coast of Peru around Christmas, as warm surface waters surge eastward and trigger changes in the climate. The fisheries of Peru are often badly affected by El Niño, because the warm water blocks a polar current that normally carries nutrient-rich water from the South Pole, on which shoals of anchovy feed.

El Niño and floods ▲

The climatic shift caused by El Niño – and by its opposite, La Niña, which often follows the next year – can cause havoc. Droughts are followed by floods, driving people from their homes and cutting food production. Droughts in the American Midwest and floods in California have both been blamed on El Niño. The effects of El Niño can be felt worldwide.

El Niño was blamed for a long drought in South Africa in 1992. Many hippopotamuses died when the water holes where they lived dried up. Some farmers tried to save them by giving them food.

El Niño and wildlife

While it brings torrential rain to Peru and Ecuador, El Niño leaves India without its monsoon rains. Bush fires and droughts caused by lack of rain kill many animals in Brazil, Indonesia, Australia, and Africa. Scientists believe that global warming is making El Niño events across the world more intense than before. Even rainforest wildlife, such as the howler monkey (above), may suffer if rain does not fall regularly.

TALKING POINT

The weather in many parts of the world is determined by ocean currents. The Gulf Stream carries warm water northeast across the Atlantic Ocean. Britain would be a much colder place without the Gulf Stream.

Q: El Niño occurs when ocean currents in the Pacific are disrupted. Could the same thing happen in the Atlantic?

A: Some scientists fear it might, if cold water from a melting Greenland ice sheet disrupted the circulation of water. This might turn off the Gulf Stream, and Britain would become as cold as Scandinavia, with spreading ice sheets in polar regions.

Rising sea levels

As the sea warms, it expands (occupies more space), which makes sea levels rise. The sea has been warming and slowly rising for about a century, but the warming is not uniform across the planet. Most warming seems to be taking place in the tropics, around the equator, where sea levels are rising fastest.

▼ Disappearing land

Sea levels rising as a result of warmer, expanding water is disastrous for people who live in the low-lying areas of places like Egypt, Bangladesh, or the Maldives. Even a rise of one foot would be catastrophic. By the middle of this century, thirty-six small island states, mainly coral islands that are barely above the sea surface, may disappear altogether. Increasingly energetic storms plus rising sea levels will produce devastating storm surges that will flood farm land with saltwater.

Coastal erosion ▲

In many places, coastlines could be eroded and many beaches could be lost. In Southeast Asia, the food needed for two hundred million people is farmed on land that could simply disappear.

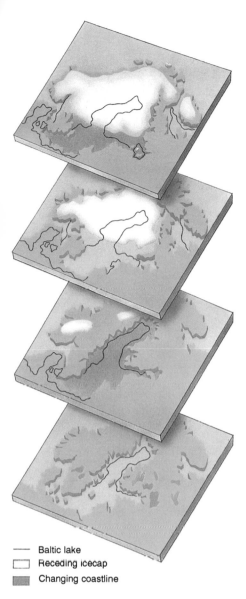

Baltic lake
Receding icecap
Changing coastline

◀ Meltdown

At the end of the last ice age, the huge icecap over Scandinavia began to melt. The vast amount of melting water led to a rise in sea levels, changing the coastline and forming the Baltic ice lake.

Polar icecaps ▶

Today, there is evidence of melting in Antarctica. Although this has been going on for seven thousand years, it is thought that global warming is speeding up the process. If the icecaps melted completely, sea levels would rise by hundreds of feet. Luckily, this is unlikely to happen because the dynamics of the ocean mean that as polar ice melts, warm sea currents are switched off. This makes the water cooler rather than warmer, so it does not expand and the sea level does not rise.

Sea defenses ▶

People have been keeping out the sea for hundreds of years. One third of the Netherlands lies below sea level, and has been captured from the sea by building dikes. In other places, huge concrete structures have been built to keep out the sea.

Reclaimed land   Dike   Sea

The most significant factor in rising sea levels is not polar icecaps melting but warmer seas in the tropics.

Q: What can be done to stop the rising sea from flooding land and ruining farming in the tropics?

A: Building dikes like the ones in the Netherlands may help in some places, but it is costly. If sea levels rise too fast, building dikes and dams may not be enough.

CHAPTER FOUR

What Is Being Done?

Alternative energy

To reduce the output of carbon dioxide – the main greenhouse gas – new sources of energy that do not depend on fossil fuels and so do not emit carbon dioxide will be needed. However, replacing coal, oil, and, eventually, natural gas is a huge task with no simple solution in sight.

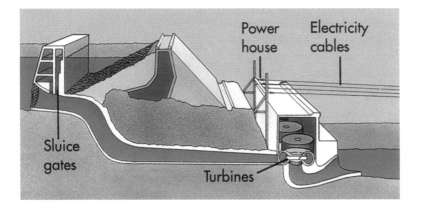

Power house

Electricity cables

Sluice gates

Turbines

◀ Water power

Hydroelectric power uses a falling stream of water to drive turbines. It works well, but needs the right conditions – a river that can be dammed to create a lake and enough falling water. In some places, trapping the incoming tide and allowing it to escape through turbines can generate power.

▼ Wind power

Wind can generate electricity, but not in large amounts. Hundreds of wind turbines would be needed to replace a single large power station.

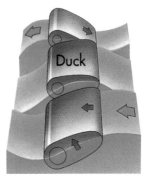

Duck

Wave power can produce more energy than tides, but it is difficult to harness. The rocking of ducks that float on the waves drives a generator, but a great number of ducks is needed to produce electricity.

The power produced by wind turbines depends on the site of the wind farm and the prevailing winds.

The wind blows around the blades of the turbines, which are connected to an electricity generator.

◄ Nuclear power

Nuclear power can produce abundant electricity without any CO_2. It is efficient and not too expensive. However, accidents at nuclear power stations in Pennsylvania, Japan, and the Ukraine – where radioactive material escaped into the atmosphere and caused widespread contamination and some deaths from radiation sickness – have made nuclear power unpopular in many places. Scientists are exploring ways of safely using another type of nuclear reaction, called fusion.

Solar power ►

The sun supplies enough energy to meet all possible needs easily – in principle. But tapping this energy is expensive because it is so spread out. Large solar panels are needed to generate power from the sun. In countries where demand is high in summer – for air-conditioning, for example – solar panels make good sense. But in countries where demand is highest in winter and the sun is not as strong, they are less practical.

Sun's rays

In a solar cell, a small electric current is produced as electric charges move between two layers of silicon.

Charge   Charge

TALKING POINT Switching away from carbon-based fuels is going to take a long time. It is not even clear yet how it can be done.

Q: Given the slow rate of changing to new energy sources, is global warming inevitable?

A: Not necessarily. Warming will continue for many years, but by slowing the growth of CO_2 production, it should be possible to limit the damage.

International cooperation

Alarmed at the dangers of global warming, the United Nations (UN) has held several international summits to set worldwide targets for reducing the amount of CO_2 emitted. The UN Intergovernmental Panel on Climate Change has declared that human dumping of CO_2 into the atmosphere is significantly changing our climate.

▲ Algae

The green weeds in the ocean, called algae, soak up a lot of CO_2. Making the algae grow better by giving them iron to feed on may encourage them to capture even more CO_2.

▲ Reforestation

Trees are excellent at absorbing carbon dioxide. Large reforestation programs could help to restore the earth's atmospheric balance. However, there may not be enough land to solve the problem this way. Trees take a very long time to grow, and, although new forests are planted, others are being destroyed at a much greater rate to use the land for farming and housing.

Climate conventions ▲

Climate conventions agreed in Brazil and Kyoto, Japan, set targets for stabilizing greenhouse gases so they do not cause dangerous shifts in the climate. By 2010 the aim is to have reduced emissions to the levels they were in 1990. Although there are no sanctions (punishment measures) against countries that fail to achieve this, many countries are making progress, spurred on by the seriousness of the problem. Public education and discussion play a major part in the international effort.

El Niño research ▶

Huge climate factors like El Niño are far too massive to control, but their effects may be forecast more accurately to enable people to take action. Most research is concentrated on understanding and predicting the process better.

By using nylon cables to anchor them to the sea bed, weather station buoys can measure ocean temperatures.

Temperature sensors

Heavy anchors

CFC free ▶

CFCs, chlorofluorocarbons, found in old refrigerators and spray cans, are greenhouse gases. They destroy the world's ozone layer, which protects us from harmful ultraviolet radiation. An international agreement is in place to phase out CFCs. This has been one of the successes of international cooperation.

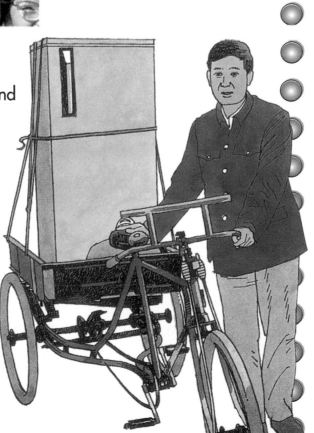

Rather than giving up fossil fuels completely, some people think it might be better to find ways of getting rid of the carbon dioxide that they produce.

Q: What other ways are there for disposing of carbon dioxide?

A: One method that has been suggested is to extract carbon dioxide from the air and pump it to the bottom of the ocean, where it would dissolve harmlessly. The energy needed to power the pump would ideally come from a nonfossil fuel source, such as solar, wind, wave, or nuclear power.

27

Look Back and Find

How much do you know about climate change? Here are some questions to test your knowledge. If you don't know any of the answers, you can find them all somewhere in the book.

The sun

What would the earth be like if it was twice as far from the sun? Obviously much colder, but would life have been possible at all on such a planet?

The sun is the key to life on Earth and the supplier of nearly all our energy. Can you think of ways in which different forms of energy rely on the sun?

Ice ages

Has the earth always had the same climate that it has today? How do we know what the climate was like in the past?

There were once great sheets of ice across northern lands. How long ago was it when they last receded, and what traces did they leave behind?

What effects might the melting of the Arctic sea ice have on climate and wildlife?

Greenhouse effect

Human beings cannot survive in extremely low temperatures, so it is fortunate for us that gases in our atmosphere warm up the planet. How much warming is there? How exactly does the greenhouse effect work? Does it happen on other planets, too?

Greenhouse gases

The atmosphere is made up mainly of nitrogen and oxygen – two gases that have no direct effect on the climate. What are the greenhouse gases that are responsible for global warming? What has been happening to greenhouse gases over the past century, as populations have grown? And how do we know?

Who is responsible?

Is everybody on the planet equally responsible for increases in greenhouse gases? We all breathe out the same amount of carbon dioxide, after all. Why do people in rich countries have so much more of an effect on the environment than those in poor countries? Why can't poor countries develop nonpolluting energy sources?

Measuring weather

How do we measure the changing temperature? What can scientists discover from looking at ice that was formed thousands of years ago?

At what rate do scientists predict that temperatures will rise? Do you think there is any room for doubt that global warming is taking place?

Sea levels

Millions of people around the world live close to river estuaries or ports. Can you think of any countries that are especially likely to be flooded if sea levels rise?

What might they do to try to protect themselves? Do you think poorer countries suffer more from flooding than richer countries? Why?

El Niño

Not all climate shifts are caused by humans. The one called El Niño has probably been going on for thousands of years.

What happens in an El Niño year? How widespread are its effects? Do you think that global warming is making the effects of El Niño worse?

Why does it matter?

Does global warming matter? After all, in many places an extra degree or so might be welcome, especially in the winter. Why don't we just let global warming happen and then make any necssary changes as we go along? What kind of weather is global warming likely to encourage?

Alternative energy

Burning fossil fuels is the basic problem that is creating a buildup of greenhouse gases in the atmosphere. But why should burning coal – which is the fossil of long-dead plants – be worse than burning wood, which people have done for thousands of years? What alternative sources of energy might we use to replace fossil fuels?

Putting it right

Once the problem of global warming was identified, international organizations and combined efforts between countries began to try to put it right. Conventions agreed on targets and goals to achieve by 2010. What are these goals and targets? Might there be alternative solutions that might cut levels of carbon dioxide in the atmosphere?

You Be Environmental!

Climate change is very hard to see or experience. Some people claim that it isn't even happening. But the majority agree that it is. What can one person do to slow down the process? The simplest thing is to avoid the wasteful use of energy. Walk or ride a bike instead of taking a car. It is much healthier, as well as gentler to the planet. Try to buy things that use less energy – if we all do that, even small savings will make a big difference.

Power stations that burn fossil fuels continue to pollute the atmosphere. Alternative energy sources need to be more fully developed and used.

Useful Addresses

Environmental Defense Fund
257 Park Avenue South
New York, NY 10010
800-684-3322
www.EDF.org

Friends of the Earth
1025 Vermont Avenue NW
Washington, DC 20005
877-843-8687
www.FOE.org

Greenpeace USA
1436 U Street NW
Washington, DC 20009
800-326-0959
www.greenpeaceusa.org

By reducing emissions of CO_2 and saving energy, we can try to reduce the damage done by the increasingly powerful storms of a globally warmed future.

International agreements

A convention to reduce greenhouse gases, agreed in Kyoto, Japan, has come into force, but how many governments take it seriously? People must keep up the pressure on politicians and vote against those who do not fulfill their pledges on climate. If we let our own comfort get in the way, the results of global warming will be suffered by our children and grandchildren.

GLOSSARY

Carbon dioxide
A gas made up of carbon and oxygen. It is formed when fuels that contain carbon (fossil fuels) are burned, and is also produced when we breathe out. Plants absorb carbon dioxide from the air and store it. Its short name is CO_2.

El Niño
A major climatic change in the Pacific Ocean, occurring every few years, in which shifts of warm water across the ocean sharply alter weather patterns. Followed by its opposite (La Niña) when the flows reverse.

Glaciers
Enormous shifting ice sheets or slow-moving rivers of ice that flow downhill.

Hurricanes
Violent storms that rotate around a central point, gaining energy from warm water on the ocean and moving slowly across it. If they reach land, their winds – of over 100 miles per hour – can do enormous damage.

Hydroelectric power
A form of electricity that is produced when a flow of water turns turbines connected to generators.

Ice sheets
Areas of ice that lie on top of solid rock, as in Greenland and Antarctica. Arctic ice is floating, so if it melts it will not add to sea level rises, but ice melting from ice sheets will.

Methane
A gas consisting of a combination of carbon and hydrogen. It is produced by rotting vegetation in marshy places and by the waste products of plant-eating animals.

Nuclear power
A form of electricity that is created in stations powered by the energy from the breaking up of atoms of heavy metals such as uranium and plutonium.

Solar cells
Cells made of silicon that convert sunlight that falls directly on them into electricity.

Temperate
The name used to describe regions of the earth that lie between the tropics and the poles.

Thermometer
An instrument used to measure temperature.

Tropics
Regions of the earth on either side of the equator. They are where global warming is thought to be having the most effect on sea levels.

Turbines
Fanlike wheels consisting of blades attached to an axle that are rotated by fluids or wind flowing past them.

Typhoons
The same as hurricanes, but occurring in the Pacific Ocean rather than the Caribbean Sea.

INDEX

A

agriculture 5, 13, 15, 19, 22, 23, 26
Antarctica 16, 23, 31
Arctic 6, 7, 28
Atlantic Ocean 21
atmosphere 5, 10, 11, 12, 13, 17, 26, 28, 29, 30

C

carbon dioxide 5, 10, 11, 12, 13, 14, 15, 16, 17, 24, 25, 26, 27, 28, 29, 30, 31
CFCs 27
CO_2 see carbon dioxide

D

deforestation 12, 13, 15, 26
drought 20, 21

E

electricity 14, 24, 25, 31
El Niño 20, 21, 27, 29, 31
emissions 14, 15, 26, 30
equator, the 9, 22, 31
erosion 22

F

farming see agriculture
flooding 20, 22, 23, 29
fossil fuel 12, 24, 27, 29, 30, 31

G

glacier 6, 7, 16, 31
global warming 4, 5, 15, 16, 17, 18, 19, 20, 21, 23, 25, 26, 28, 29, 30, 31
greenhouse effect 10, 11, 28
greenhouse gases 10, 11, 12, 14, 17, 24, 26, 27, 28, 29, 30
Gulf Stream, the 21

H

heatwave 9
helium 8, 10
hurricane 18, 31
hydroelectric power 24, 31
hydrogen 8, 9, 31

I

ice ages 6, 8, 10, 17, 18, 23, 28
icecap 6, 23
ice sheet 6, 16, 21, 28, 31
industry 5, 12, 13, 14, 15

M

methane 10, 12, 31
migration 16

N

nitrogen 10, 28
nuclear power 25, 27, 31

O

oxygen 8, 9, 10, 11, 13, 28, 31
ozone 10, 27

P

Pacific Ocean 20, 21, 31
plants 8, 9, 11, 13, 15, 16, 29, 31
pollution 5, 9, 14, 28

R

rainfall 7, 9, 11, 21

S

satellite 17
sea ice 7, 28
sea level 5, 6, 22, 23, 29, 31

seasons

seasons 4, 9
smog 5, 14
solar cells 25, 31
solar power 25, 27
solar radiation 8, 11, 27
Stevenson screen 16
storm 4, 19, 20, 22, 30, 31
stratosphere 17

T

temperate region 9, 19, 31
thermometer 16, 31
tropics, the 22, 23, 31
turbine 24, 31
typhoon see hurricane

U

ultraviolet radiation 27

W

water vapor 8, 10, 11
wave power 24, 27
weather stations 16, 17, 27
wind 18, 20, 24
wind power 24, 27

⚫ ⚫

Picture Credits

Abbreviations: t-top, b-bottom, c-center, r-right, l-left.

Cover & Pages 5, 9, 13, 14, 15c, 17, 18, 20 both, 21, 22c, 25 & 26-27 – Frank Spooner Pictures.
4, 12, 19 & 23 – Eye Ubiquitous. 7, 15b, 22b, 24 & 26c – Spectrum Color Library.
8 & 16 – Oxford Scientific Films. 26t – Bruce Coleman Collection. 6-7 – Flick Killerby.